WE HAVE A POPE

2,000 YEARS OF PRESERVING THE FAITH

Stephen K. Ray
R. Dennis Walters

CATHOLIC ANSWERS
San Diego
2005

We Have a Pope: 2,000 Years of Preserving the Faith published by
CATHOLIC ANSWERS, INC.
P. O. Box 199000, San Diego, California 92159-9000
(888) 291-8000 (U.S. orders)
(619) 387-0042 (fax)
www.catholic.com (web)

Copyright © 2005 by Catholic Answers

All rights reserved. Except for quotations, no part of this book may be reproduced or transmitted in any form or by any means, electronic or mechanical, including photocopying, recording, uploading to the Internet, or by any information storage and retrieval system, without written permission from the publisher.

Unless otherwise noted, Scripture quotations taken from the Revised Standard Version: Catholic Edition (RSV:CE) of the Bible, copyright © 1996 by Division of Christian Education of the National Council of the Churches of Christ in the United States of America.

*Nihil Obstat: I have concluded that the materials
presented in this work are free of doctrinal and moral errors.
Monsignor Robert Lunsford, censor librorum
July 21, 2003*

*Imprimatur: permission to publish this work is granted.
Bishop Carl F. Mengeling, Diocese of Lansing
July 21, 2003*

Cover design by Devin Schadt   Book design by Claudine and Company
Printed in the United States of America   ISBN: 1-888992-91-3

A Protestant woman visiting St. Peter's Basilica in 1975 recalled: "There are no pews there. Everybody stands for everything. I was there with hundreds of people waiting for the pope, and was standing somewhere in the middle of the nave.

"Now, I wasn't much interested in the pope or in Catholic things. I was with a tour group. I'm pretty short, and couldn't see anything except the shoulders of those in front of me.

"All of a sudden, flashbulbs started going off near the entrance to the basilica, and the light was reflected off the ceiling. I watched as the flashes got nearer, and then I caught a glimpse of this thin little man being carried on a platform with a chair by four strapping guys. I began to feel prickly all over; all the hair on my neck and arms was standing on end. It was a reaction I didn't expect.

"When he was right in front of me, I realized I was staring at the history of the Church."

Why Do We Need a Pope?

Many Christians of all persuasions recognize the pope as a symbol of something they yearn for. He represents unity, fullness, and stability—the qualities Jesus prayed his Church would possess. "And I have given them the glory you gave me, so that they may be one, as we are one, I in them and you in me, that they may be brought to perfection as one, that the world may know that you sent me, and that you loved them even as you loved me" (John 17:22–23, New American Bible [NAB]).

Seeing the pope as this kind of symbol is good, but he is more than that. If the pope were nothing more than a symbol, we wouldn't really need him. A symbol points to an ideal such as holiness or unity. But the pope is more than simply a signpost. God gives him a real job to do. Without his leadership, the Catholic Church would certainly suffer the same tendency to divide and compete that other Christian groups do. Without his leadership, the one, holy, catholic, and apostolic Church that Jesus founded would disintegrate.

According to the *World Christian Encyclopedia*, by the year 2000 Christians outside the Catholic Church had split into over 33,000 denominations. This disunity is not what Jesus intended for his people. The Church was not meant to be fractured, any more than a human body is meant to be broken into pieces (see 1 Cor. 1:10). As the experience of such groups shows, without the pope, the teaching passed down from the apostles would be transformed into all sorts of fanciful, ideological, or political shapes. Many people would drift away from Jesus Christ on secular currents.

Who Instituted the Papacy?

When the public of his day was abuzz with speculation about who Jesus might be and how he might figure in God's plan, Jesus asked his disciples, "Who do men say that the Son of Man is?" After various answers, he asked them, "Who do you say that I am?" Simon said, "You are the Christ, the Son of the living God." Jesus replied, "Flesh and blood has not revealed this to you, but my Father who is in heaven." Jesus then addressed Simon personally and said: "I tell you, you are Peter [Greek, *petros*], and on this rock [Greek, *petra*] I will build my Church, and the powers of death shall not prevail against it. I will give you the keys of the kingdom of heaven, and whatever you bind on earth shall be bound in heaven, and whatever you loose on earth shall be loosed in heaven" (Matt. 16:13–19).

In this passage, Jesus instituted the papacy.

Some Christians dispute that interpretation. Jesus, they might point out, didn't use the word *pope*, and Peter didn't call himself a "pope"; in fact, you can't even find the word *pope* in the Bible.

True—but beside the point.

The point is not what Peter *called* himself, but what he *did*. He was an apostle among other apostles—a bishop among other bishops—but did he actually *use* the "keys of the kingdom of heaven"? Did he exercise the office as leader of the entire Church as it existed then, and did he pass that office on to successors? Let's look at these questions in detail, starting with Peter himself.

Why Peter?

Ask someone to describe Simon Peter during the time Jesus walked the earth, and you're likely to get a picture of a buffoon who put his foot in his mouth, misunderstood the simplest parables, and even lied to protect himself. It's hard to imagine why Jesus would have called such a man "Rock" and given him the keys to anything.

But there is another side to Peter. He is a businessman and a natural leader. As a commercial fisherman, he had partners and owned several boats. He owned a home in Capernaum where Jesus stayed (Mark 1:29–33, 2:1–2). Peter was industrious, devoutly religious, and capable of admitting his own sinfulness (Luke 5:8). He would stick his neck out when others were afraid to (Matt. 14:28–29), and was even willing to leave everything behind to follow Jesus (Matt 4:19–20).

Peter is always mentioned first in lists of Jesus' disciples (for example, Matt. 10:2, Mark 3:16, Luke 6:14, and Acts 1:13) while, interestingly enough, Judas Iscariot is always listed last. Peter frequently speaks for the group (Matt. 16:16, John 6:68–69), and is the only one who walked to Jesus on the water (Matt. 14:29). More important, Jesus gives Peter alone the keys (Matt.

16:19). He tells Peter at the Last Supper that he will pray for him so that Peter will then strengthen his brothers (Luke 22:32). And after the Resurrection, Jesus commands Peter to "feed my lambs" and "tend my sheep" (John 21:15–17).

What's So Important about a Name Change?

People use nicknames to describe a person's appearance (Curly) or characteristics (Smiley). But new names were much more significant for ancient people than they are today. Name changes of this sort indicated a change of role or status.

For example, in Genesis, God changes Abram's name to Abraham, to emphasize his new role as a "father of a multitude of nations" (Gen. 17:5). Pharaoh changes the patriarch Joseph's name when he is designated as vizier, or chief steward (Gen. 41:45).

Seemingly highlighting the point of Peter's name change, Matthew records that the event took place at Caesarea Philippi (16:13), the location of an enormous rock cliff. Jesus spoke Aramaic, and would have used the Aramaic word for rock, *kçpha*: "You are *kçpha*, and on this *kçpha* I will build my Church." When this statement was brought into Greek, some New Testament writers used a variant of *kçpha* that had been adapted slightly: *Kçphas* (or *Cephas* in most English Bibles).

Most of the time, however, the name was simply translated: *petros,* from which we get "Peter" in English. This is the most common way he is referred to in the New Testament, but sometimes New Testament writers still use *Cephas.* Paul is one of the writers who does this (1 Cor. 15:5, Gal. 1:18), and in so doing he acknowledges the name change and unique office.

The name change refers to more than a personality trait. Matthew explicitly connects it with a change of Peter's role and status: "On this rock I will build. . . . I will give you the keys. . . . Whatever you bind on earth. . . . Whatever you loose on earth . . ." (Matt. 16:18–19). In other words, Jesus was giving Peter *authority*—an office.

What Authority Did Peter Have?

Authority is usually signified by an emblem or symbol. With Joseph, it was the king's own signet ring (Gen. 41:42). For the chief stewards of the kings of Judah, the emblem for such authority was a key that sometimes was carried on the shoulder.

Isaiah tells of Eliakim, who replaced another steward: "I will call my servant Eliakim the son of Hilkiah, and I will clothe him with your robe, and will bind your girdle on him, and will commit your authority to his hand; and he shall be a father to the inhabitants of Jerusalem and to the house of Judah. And I will place on his shoulder the key of the house of David; he shall open, and none shall shut; and he shall shut, and none shall open" (Is. 22:20–22).

This key symbolized the authority that the steward had over the kingdom. By the king's command, the steward could dispense or withhold favor, and grant or deny opportunity. Isaiah 22 is the Old Testament background for Matthew 16:19.

In Matthew 16, Jesus uses the image of keys to symbolize the extent of Peter's authority over the "kingdom of heaven" (the Church). The keys given to the chief steward symbolized an authority second only to the king's. To emphasize his point, Jesus added: "Whatever you bind on earth shall be bound in heaven, and whatever you loose on earth shall be loosed in heaven" (Matt. 16:19). The other apostles shared a like authority under the headship of Peter (Matt. 18:18), but Peter alone was invested with the keys according to Matthew.

In Jesus' day, the expression "bind and loose" applied to the authority held by Jewish leaders. They could include or exclude from the community, and punish or absolve—that is, they held both a legislative and a judicial authority. Jesus gave Peter that authority in his kingdom.

Who Actually Led the Early Church?

Peter's authority was more than simply a matter of honor, as becomes clear after Jesus' Ascension into heaven.

Acts 1–15 describes Peter's singular leadership of the fledgling Church in Jerusalem. He began immediately to act as spokesman for the entire group of disciples. Speaking for the new Church, he preached repentance, faith, and baptism (Acts 2:14 ff., 3:11 ff.). To the Sanhedrin, Peter explained the meaning of a healing (Acts 4:8–12), and twice refused to stop preaching the name of Jesus (Acts 4:19–20, 5:29–32).

Peter also assumed leadership of the day-to-day life of the Jerusalem Church. He determined the need to fill the vacated office of Judas (Acts 1:15 ff.). He became the focus of many of the signs and wonders that took place (Acts 5:15). He guided daily Church life, the meetings for teaching and prayer, and even public discipline (Acts 5:1–11). Of the twelve original apostles, only his words are recorded in the book of Acts.

As the Church began to spread, Peter exercised binding and loosing authority. He completed the initiation of the Samaritan converts, and rebuked Simon the Magician for trying to buy spiritual gifts (Acts 8:14–24). Without consulting the other apostles, he opened baptism and salvation to the Gentiles (Acts 10) and resisted pressure to reconsider (Acts 11:1–18). That decision and his theological pronouncement in Acts 15 guided the Jerusalem council to continue to admit non-Jews into the Church without circumcising them first (Acts 15:7–12).

Because of persecutions and the rapid expansion of the Church, Peter moved to Syrian Antioch, the first major center of Gentile Christianity (Gal. 2:11). Later, as the gospel spread westward, he moved west, traveling and preaching in Asia Minor, through Corinth, and finally to Rome, from where he wrote a letter to the Asian churches (1 Pet. 1:1, 5:13). From there he continued to lead the universal Church until his death.

Rome, Not Jerusalem or Antioch

History indicates that Peter headed the Church at Jerusalem for about ten years, and at Antioch for about a year. Yet the final seat of Peter's authority is at Rome. Why?

Peter most likely arrived in Rome during the reign of Emperor Claudius, probably around A.D. 42, and left the city when Claudius expelled Jews in 49. Peter was back in Jerusalem for the council in Acts 15, then journeyed through Asia Minor and returned to Rome in 54 (after Claudius died), leaving again on a missionary journey around 57. By A.D. 62, he was back in Rome, and in 67 was martyred under Nero.

How do we know of Peter's Roman sojourns and his

death in that city? Because Church Fathers as early as Clement of Rome (writing during the apostle John's lifetime) uniformly attest that Peter ministered and died in Rome. For a few examples, Irenaeus (died c. 200) says that Peter and Paul died there, and Tertullian (died c. 225) states casually that Peter baptized in the Tiber River, which flows through Rome. According to Church historian Eusebius (c. 260–c. 340), Peter served as bishop of Rome for twenty-five years and was martyred there. Archaeologists have determined that Peter was buried in a graveyard on Vatican Hill, where Constantine built the first St. Peter's Basilica over Peter's grave.

The papacy is based on the phenomenon of "apostolic succession," by which the governing of the Church descended from the apostles onto their successors, the bishops. In a special way, Peter's office as the Church's highest earthly leader was passed on to his successors, the bishops of Rome. When Peter left the East for Rome, his authority traveled with him. It remained with the church he was heading at the time of his death, where his first successor, Linus, was appointed. According to Irenaeus, Paul makes mention of this Linus in his letters to Timothy (*Against Heresies*).

How Do We Know That Peter Had Successors?

Many Protestants accept that Peter enjoyed special authority among the disciples, but not that Jesus intended for him to pass this authority on to others. Scripture and history indicate otherwise.

Isaiah makes it clear that the office of the chief steward in Judah was passed on, as we saw in Isaiah when the key was passed on (Is. 22:20–22).

The apostles themselves appointed their successors, the bishops. Part of Paul's ministry was to appoint elders to administer the churches (Acts 14:23). He tells Timothy and Titus to appoint bishops, even describing the kinds of men they should appoint (1 Tim. 3:1–13, Titus 1:5–9).

Extra-biblical evidence confirms apostolic succession. Clement of Rome, who was himself the third successor of Peter, wrote to the Corinthian church sometime around A.D. 96: "From their earliest converts [the apostles] appointed men whom they had tested by the Spirit to act as bishops and deacons for the future believers. . . . Our apostles, too, were given to understand by our Lord Jesus Christ that the office of bishop would give rise to intrigues. For this reason, equipped as they were with perfect foreknowledge, they appointed the men mentioned before, and afterward laid down a rule once for all to this effect: when these men die, other approved men shall succeed to their sacred ministry" (*Epistle to the Corinthians* 44).

From the beginning, the Church kept lists of those who succeeded to Peter's office. To date, there have been 264. Incidentally, the current pope is *not* simply the successor of the previous pope. He is the successor of Peter the apostle. So John Paul II as the 264th bishop of Rome was the 263rd successor of Peter.

How Were Successors Chosen?

We know how Peter was chosen to lead the Church: Jesus appointed him as any king would appoint his chief steward. The first few popes may have been directly appointed by their predecessors; by the second century, however, an election process had developed.

Selecting the pope meant selecting the bishop of Rome, so the election was restricted to Rome and its vicinity. Many Christians in Rome and the surrounding region were involved, including neighboring bishops, Roman clergy, and even laity. The clergy would choose a candidate, and the laity would affirm the choice by acclamation. Though modified by Leo I after A.D. 440, that process was essentially the one used until about the tenth century.

Pope Nicholas II eventually made the cardinals (key members of the clergy of Rome) responsible for the election. Occasionally, this took awhile if the cardinals couldn't quickly agree on a candidate. The longest papal election took nearly three years (1268–1271). Frustrated, the citizens tore the roof off the meeting hall, locked the cardinals inside, and restricted them to a diet of bread and water. They quickly elected Gregory X.

That solution created the *conclave,* a closed meeting of the College of Cardinals for the purpose of electing a pope. With some adjustments, it's still the method used today.

When a pope dies, a cardinal—the papal chamberlain—summons eligible cardinals to Rome. The conclave convenes in the Sistine Chapel, starting with the hymn *Veni, Creator Spiritus* ("Come, Creator Spirit"). The cardinals write the name of a candidate on a paper ballot and personally deposit it in a special chalice. It takes a two-thirds majority to elect. If a pope is not elected on the first try, the ballots are burned in such a way that the smoke ascending through the chimney shows black. The cardinals then proceed to the next ballot.

With a final two-thirds majority, the chamberlain asks the elected cardinal if he accepts the election and, if so, what name he wishes to take. The new pope assumes office the moment he accepts. Then the ballots are burned so that the smoke is white—the world then knows we have a new pope!

What Does Papal Primacy Mean?

The question naturally arises: If the pope is the bishop of Rome, why does he have primacy over the whole Church?

In brief, it is because he is the successor of Peter and has Peter's authority. Though Peter was one apostle among the Twelve and had the same apostolic authority they had, he was given a unique authority that the others were not.

Though this isn't as clear in the English text of Matthew's Gospel, it is very clear in the Greek that Jesus is singling out Peter for a special role. Standard English has no way to distinguish between "you" used to refer to just one person and "you" referring to several people, but Greek does. In Greek, "you [singular]" and "you [plural]" are different. In Matthew 16, Jesus tells Peter, "I will give you [singular] the keys of the kingdom of heaven, and whatever you [singular] bind on earth shall be bound in heaven, and whatever you [singular] loose on earth shall be loosed in heaven" (Matt. 16:19). Two chapters later, Jesus says something similar when he commissions the rest of the apostles: "Truly, I say to you [plural], whatever you [plural] bind on earth shall be bound in heaven, and whatever you [plural] loose on earth shall be loosed in heaven" (Matt. 18:18).

But there's a key omission in the latter passage (pun intended). Jesus gives Peter alone the power of the keys.

Only one person has possession of those keys—the chief steward, Peter. Although all of the Twelve are given the power to bind and loose, Jesus is shown giving the keys to Peter alone (Matt. 16:19).

As we saw earlier, Peter recognized that his decisions applied to both Jewish and Gentile Christians, and needed no prior approval from others. Acts relates that Peter, responding to a vision from heaven, went to the home of a Gentile named Cornelius, preached the gospel to his household, and then baptized them (Acts 10). Criticized by Jewish Christians who insisted upon circumcision, Peter explained himself without seeking approval or apologizing (Acts 11:1–18). Later, at the Council of Jerusalem, Peter reaffirmed this decision. James supported the decision, and suggested how to implement it (Acts 15:4–21).

From the earliest years of the Church, popes have recognized that their primacy succeeded from Peter. It was not merely a position of honor, but carried real authority.

Of many examples, one will do. Eutyches, a fifth-century Greek monk, taught that the humanity of Jesus was swallowed up in his divinity at the moment of the Incarnation. Flavian, patriarch of Constantinople, denounced Eutyches as a heretic. Both sides appealed to Leo I in Rome. Leo's reply came in the form of a long letter (called *The Tome of Leo*), upholding the orthodox teaching that Jesus has both a divine and a human nature. Leo expected this letter to settle the issue. When it was finally read at the council of Eastern bishops, they shouted, "Peter has spoken through Leo."

Did the Early Church Think the Pope Had Primacy?

Matthew's Gospel made it clear that Jesus had given Peter an office (symbolized by the keys) that included authority to bind and loose (Matt. 16:19). Jesus gave other apostles also the power to bind and loose (Matt. 18:18), but he gave the keys to Peter alone. John's Gospel repeats the point: Jesus gave *all* the apostles authority to forgive or retain sins (John 20:23), but he gave Peter *alone* the authority to govern and teach the whole flock (21:15–17). The early popes recognized the authority that came to them from Peter, but did the rest of the Church recognize it as well?

In a word—yes. Three quick examples:

Irenaeus of Lyons, writing around A.D. 180, says the apostles Peter and Paul founded the church of Rome, and its authority has been handed down from them. "For it is a matter of necessity that every church should agree with this church [Rome], on account of its preeminent authority" (*Against Heresies* 3,3,2).

Cyprian of Carthage, writing around A.D. 251: "If someone does not hold fast to this unity of Peter, can he imagine that he still holds the faith? If he desert the chair of Peter upon whom the Church was built, can he still be confident that he is in the Church?" (*The Unity of the Catholic Church* 4).

Jerome, translator of the Bible, wrote to Pope Damasus I: "I think it my duty to consult the chair of Peter, and to turn to a church [Rome] whose faith has been praised by Paul. I appeal for spiritual food to the church whence I have received the garb of Christ" (Letter 15).

Do the *actions* of early bishops back up such words? Again, yes. First, the bishop of Rome often intervened in a local church's affairs, as Clement I did at Corinth. No one challenged his right to do so. Second, individual bishops looked to Rome as the guardian of orthodoxy, as Cyprian of Carthage did in the third century against local heretics.

What About the Pope's Titles?

The word *pope* is an English form of the Greek word *pappas*, "papa" or "father." According to Isaiah 22:21, the chief steward was "a father to the inhabitants of Jerusalem." Paul referred to himself as a father (e.g., 1 Cor. 4:15), and many bishops of the early Church were called "pope." In the eleventh century, Gregory VII reserved the title to the bishop of Rome.

The pope has a number of titles. One of them is simply "Bishop of Rome" because that's exactly what he is, bishop of the diocese of Rome.

The pope is also called "Patriarch of the West." The Catholic Church contains a number of different "rites" or ritual churches in union with the pope. Most of these rites are Eastern. Each is headed by a bishop called a patriarch, such as the patriarch of the Byzantine Church. As Patriarch of the West, the pope is head of the Latin Church, by far the largest ritual Church within the Catholic Church.

A third title is "Vicar of Christ." A *vicar* is a deputy, a person who represents someone else, as an ambassador represents the king. The pope represents Christ to the world, which is why Pope Innocent III adopted Vicar of Christ as an official title.

Two of the more interesting titles are "Supreme Pontiff" and "Servant of the Servants of God."

A *pontiff* is a builder of bridges. The title originally belonged to the Roman emperors, who saw themselves as the bridge between their subjects and the gods. Once the emperors were Christians, they recognized that they did not play this role. In 375, Emperor Gratian applied that title to Pope Damasus I as the bridge builder for the true God. The pope's job is to take the lead in bridging the gap between mankind and Christ: he presents the Church to Christ and Christ to the Church.

Pope Gregory I (590–604) preferred to call himself the "Servant of the Servants of God." Popes see their office as a service and a ministry to other bishops and to the Church at large. This was Gregory's favorite title, because it captured the heart of the papacy. The title Servant of the Servants of God is usually mentioned last on the list but it is the title that expresses the attitude in which the pope is to conduct his office.

What Does the Pope Do?

From well before sunrise until well after dark, the pope is busy with a mountain of tasks. They fall into three main categories.

First, teaching. The pope must ensure that what the early Church heard from the lips of Jesus and the Twelve is the same message it's hearing today, two thousand years later. And he has to make sure that same message gets passed on to future generations. This is not an easy job because times change, understanding grows, and the whole Church worldwide needs to hear the message. Also, the Church consists of people from many cultures, speaking many languages yet the pope must effectively teach each of them. Further, people often want to "adjust" the gospel to suit themselves, and the pope has to be sure that teaching remains consistent with the truth. So teaching is a Priority One task.

Second, governing. Of course, the pope does head up a tiny state called Vatican City, but that's not his ultimate governing role. The pope governs the Church, making sure that the worldwide Church has what it needs to fulfill its mission of preaching Jesus Christ and his gift of salvation everywhere. Working with the bishops, the pope has overall responsibility for the spiritual welfare of over a billion Catholics. Again, a difficult, demanding, and crucial job.

Third, sanctifying. Though the Holy Spirit is the ultimate sanctifier of the Church, his ministers strive to help Christians cooperate with the sanctifying action of the Spirit. One way popes do this is by striving to be models of personal holiness. They also ensure that the sacraments are celebrated properly. They negotiate with governments to protect the freedom of all Christians to worship and practice their faith. They explain, protect, and encourage Catholics to practice Christian morality. And they work to make sure that the Church is protected from the influence of what the Bible calls "false brethren," Catholics and non-Catholic Christians who would draw the faithful into error.

Do Catholics Always Have to Agree with the Pope?

The pope is commissioned to teach infallibly but he does not always teach that way. He can teach infallibly in two broad categories: faith and morals. The pope can teach what Christians are to believe and how they are to live out their Christian lives morally. The flip side is that the pope sometimes must teach Christians what they should *not* believe, and what they must *not* do. An example may illustrate this point.

Pope John Paul II published a letter about Catholic moral doctrine, called *Veritatis Splendor* (The Splendor of Truth). Though not itself infallible, this encyclical underscored important and binding truths. He wrote it because the world is facing a crisis of moral truth—it no longer believes that there is such a thing. "You have your truth, and I have mine" is not Catholic teaching (or good logic!). The pope wanted to explain the basis for morality from Scripture and reason. He also needed to warn Catholics about false moral approaches. For example, he stressed the scriptural principle that one may not do evil so that good can come from it (Rom. 3:8).

Most papal teaching (in audiences, homilies, and written documents) does not claim to be infallible (guaranteed free of error). However, even in these cases Catholics must presume that he is teaching correctly. They are not free to simply disregard his teaching because it has not been promulgated infallibly. If they have questions, they still owe the pope "the benefit of the doubt," and the more strongly the pope has taught something, the more strongly Catholics are obligated to give weight to what he has said. When he exercises the fullness of his authority as the successor of Peter and teaches infallibly, they are bound to accept the teaching as protected by

God from error.

This pertains to what the pope says regarding matters of faith and morals and those truths needed to explain and defend matters of faith and morals. It does not apply to truths in other areas. The pope may be a competent scientist, philosopher, politician, or economist. But when he speaks about these things, it is possible to disagree with him. Popes have even disagreed with other popes about the right way to handle political situations.

Only when science, philosophy, politics, or economics intrudes into the realm of faith and morals can the pope speak about it authoritatively. For example, the Christian faith teaches that the universe was created from nothing by God. This does not tell us anything about how old the cosmos is or how God brought about the life-forms in the universe—whether he used evolution or not. On all those matters one is free to hold various views. However, the faith does teach that in the beginning God made the world from nothing, and the pope is qualified to teach authoritatively about that.

Infallibility

From time to time—but not often—the pope speaks infallibly. That is, what he says is protected by God to be free of error. The pope's ability to do this is based on

Scripture.

Earlier, we learned that Jesus gave Peter a position of authority, granting him the "power of the keys" with authority to "bind and loose" (cf. Matt. 16:19). What Peter declared on earth, God would ratify in heaven! This meant that God would have to superintend (oversee) Peter's words. We also learned that Jesus charged Peter to strengthen his fellow apostles in their faith (Luke 22:32) and to "feed my sheep" (John 21:17)—both references to a teaching and governing authority. But Jesus said more.

At the Last Supper, he promised the Twelve that he would send the Holy Spirit to lead them into the truth (John 16:13). Jesus taught the truth because he *is* the truth (John 14:6). Because the Spirit of truth (not mere human insight) would lead the apostles (John 16:13–15), Jesus commissioned the Twelve to speak for God. In response, the people were required to listen with all attentiveness and obedience.

Infallibility is a gift granted not to Peter alone nor to the Twelve personally, nor even to their successors, but to the Church as a whole. It is the Church, after all, that is the "pillar and bulwark of the truth" (1 Tim. 3:15). The pope *participates* in that infallibility in a unique way.

Long before infallibility was formally defined in 1870, the Fathers and Doctors of the Church understood that what popes taught about faith and morals was final. In the thirteenth century, Thomas Aquinas held that the pope "is empowered to decide matters of faith finally, so that they may be held by all with unshaken faith" (*Summa Theologiae* II–II:1:10).

So when the First Vatican Council (1870) defined papal infallibility, it was already the faith of the Church and had been down through history. In fact, the doctrine that the pope could speak infallibly was not under discussion at the Council. It was recognized by all. The Council dealt with the *manner* in which the pope speaks infallibly.

According to the Council: "When the Roman pontiff speaks *ex cathedra*, that is, when, in the exercise of his office as shepherd and teacher of all Christians, in virtue of his supreme apostolic authority, he defines a doctrine concerning faith or morals to be held by the whole Church, he possesses, by the divine assistance promised to him in blessed Peter, that infallibility which the divine Redeemer willed his Church to enjoy in defining doctrine concerning faith or morals" (*Pastor Aeternus* 4).

The basic affirmation here is that when the pope "speaks *ex cathedra* . . . he possesses . . . that infallibility which the divine Redeemer willed his Church to enjoy in defining doctrine concerning faith or morals." *Ex cathedra* is Latin for "from the chair." The idea is that the pope is infallible when he speaks "from the chair" of Peter, which is to say, with the fullness of his authority as Peter's successor.

The Council tells us that the pope speaks *ex cathedra* "when, in the exercise of his office as shepherd and teacher of all Christians, in virtue of his supreme apostolic authority, he defines a doctrine concerning faith or morals to be held by the whole Church." The pope therefore invokes the fullness of his authority as Peter's successor. He is not acting as a private theologian, as bishop of Rome, as patriarch of the West, or even in his ordinary teaching capacity as pope.

Once a doctrine has been defined, it is no longer legitimate to question or dispute it. The pope is given authority to teach the Christian faith. The primary objects of his infallibility are the subjects of faith and morals, though infallibility can also be brought to bear on related matters needed to defend and explain matters of faith and morals. Finally, because the matter has been defined for all, it is to be held "by the whole Church."

Most of the time, even when the pope speaks with great solemnity, he does not engage his infallibility, but sometimes he does. Two recent doctrines that the pope did proclaim infallibly are Mary's Immaculate Conception (defined by Pius IX in 1854) and her Assumption into heaven (defined by Pius XII in 1950).

If Popes Sin, How Can We Trust What They Say?

It's clear what infallibility *is*. Unfortunately, people sometimes confuse it with a few things that it *isn't*.

For example, infallibility isn't the same as *inspiration*. Scripture is *inspired* because what the authors have written is "God-breathed"—God is the primary author of Scripture. Inspiration is a positive action of the Holy Spirit. On the other hand, infallibility is something negative, a guarantee that something is *not* in error. The Church makes no claim that what the pope says is inspired, or timely, or stylistically readable. It only claims that the definition (as far as it goes) is not wrong. Infallibility is a *protective* mechanism that guards against error—a very important distinction.

Infallibility also doesn't mean that the pope is *impeccable* (unable to sin). Peter called himself a sinful man (Luke 5:8), and did in fact sin by denying Jesus (John 18:17). Yet Jesus gave Peter a teaching office that heaven itself would ratify. The charism of infallibility doesn't protect the pope from sin, only from officially teaching error. Sinlessness is not required.

Should the Pope Matter to Non-Catholics?

Actually, the pope matters a great deal to members of other Christian traditions, and even other religions.

As we saw earlier, Protestant communions frequently split over "irreconcilable differences," some significant, some trivial. Even among Eastern Orthodox churches, divisions occur along national, ethnic, or political lines. Such divisions are not what Jesus had in mind when he prayed "that they may become perfectly one, so that the world may know that thou hast sent me and hast loved them even as thou hast loved me" (John 17:23).

The pope matters to non-Catholic Christians because he stands as a visible source of unity, the practical answer to Jesus' prayer for unity. He also stands for the very thing that enables the world to know that Jesus is for real: "By this all men will know that you are my disciples, if you have love for one another" (John 13:35).

The pope matters to members of non-Christian religions as well. Christianity places Catholics in a special relation with the Jews. Recent popes have condemned anti-Semitism in all its forms and worked tirelessly to repair damaged relations between the two religions.

The popes have also begun to talk with Muslim leaders in an effort to promote peace and work together against secularist threats, such as the anti-family agenda common in the United Nations bureaucracy. Popes have also worked with leaders of other religions for the mutual understanding of what we have in common. This understanding not only promotes greater harmony but also serves as a "preparation for the gospel" that in the future can draw members of other religions to the faith of Christ.

The pope matters even to nonreligious people. He is, after all, head of a small but influential state. He can and does affect the outcome of world events. Historians believe John Paul II's influence accelerated the fall of Communism in Europe.

The pope matters to people of every stripe.

Why the Pope Should Matter to You

So, what does a pope in far-off Rome have to do with you? For Catholics, the pope's leadership colors everything about the faith they profess and the way they live it.

The Church today faithfully teaches what it has always taught. The language in which the faith is formulated has developed, understanding of its riches has deepened, and the Church has grown. But what Catholics believe now about the nature of Christ, the Holy Trinity, grace, salvation, the sacraments, and eternal life they believe because of the authority and guidance of the pope through the centuries and the bishops in union with him.

The Church today also worships as it always has. The languages of worship have changed and multiplied but the Scripture the Church reads and the sacraments it celebrates still exist because of the guidance of the pope and the bishops in union with him.

The moral standards of the Christian life are taught today as they always have been. Times have changed, and so have manners and customs but the morals of family life, the practice of virtue, the call to holiness—all these are preserved because of the pope and the bishops in union with him.

All of these things have direct bearing on your life, whether you are already a Catholic or are someone responding to God's call to enter the fullness of truth and grace that is found within his Son's Church.

During 2,000 years of Christian history, kingdoms have come and gone. Institutions have appeared and disappeared. Peoples have come together, and have scattered. The Catholic Church has remained since it was founded by Christ, under the leadership of his representative, the pope. The papacy, *the oldest existing office in the world*, stretches back in a continual line to St. Peter.

This could not have happened unless God had willed it. Jesus himself said it—Jesus, who is true to his promises: "I tell you, you are Peter, and on this rock I will build my Church, and the powers of death shall not prevail against it" (Matt. 16:18). That Church still stands on that rock—Peter and his successors.